THE POWER TO CONNECT®

Creating communication that gets results

Teresa Easler
Chuck Easler
with Mark Cosgrove

Teresa Easler
Chuck Easler
with Mark Cosgrove
Power to Connect®
Corporate Vision Communication Inc.

Published by Motivated Publishing Ventures

ISBN 0-9732657-0-1
Printed in Canada
First Edition: February 2003

Acknowledgements

To Dan Sullivan and Babs Smith, for your trust, friendship, several good kicks in the pants, and far more than we can ever express.

To Stewert Emery & Carol Augustus, for all you taught us about human interactions, possibilities, and self expression.

To Roger Ailes, you taught us that "we are the message".

To our staff at Corporate Vision, for your support, honesty, and passion to learn.

To our clients for teaching us so much about communication and excellence.

To Casey Combden and his team, for a short deadline and for providing "roads and trucks".

II Acknowledgements

For Alex and Carter, the best kids anyone could want, for your aliveness, courage, and for constantly teaching us new things.

To Chuck, my partner in life and business, for your brilliance in seeing what no one else can and for always loving me.

To my life partner Teresa, for her love and inspiration.

Table of Contents

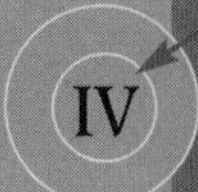
IV

Foreword

I'd like to tell you a story. Back in 1982, I had this great desire to improve my ability to communicate, both in one-to-one situations, and in presentation situations. I heard about this program that was supposed to provide dramatic improvements, and I signed up immediately. It started on a Friday night and went until late Sunday afternoon. During approximately twenty hours of workshop time I went through some very grueling processes, many of them asking me to bare my soul and to stop hiding my true self. There was a lot of way-out theory about why people don't communicate, and I found myself surrounded in the program by a lot of people that I didn't really like. We finished on Sunday afternoon being told that we had all made real breakthroughs and that we would start seeing some remarkable results in our life.

But a month later, I couldn't remember any of the theories, the processes had faded, and I didn't notice much improvement in my ability to communicate.

Being a bear for punishment, I heard about another program which was supposed to be "absolutely revolutionary" in the results it produced. A lot more grueling exercises and weird theories, but a month later no big change in my results.

After that, I decided that the only way I was going to become a better communicator was by constantly throwing myself into situations where I had to communicate to audiences. I did this for the next dozen years and what I noticed is that I certainly had a big increase in my confidence about speaking, but I still felt there was a big skill missing. More than that, I began to feel that I didn't even know how to think about speaking, didn't even know how to prepare my mind and my message for a particular situation. Some of my speeches were good, some of them missed the mark -- and I didn't know what made the difference.

You need to realize that all of this time I was becoming more successful in my business. Yet I had this sense that a dramatic increase in my ability to communicate would also lead to dramatic increase in my success.

That's where Teresa and Chuck Easler entered my life. In 1996, I attended a two-day workshop where I learned how to use and apply their **Power to Connect** concepts, and especially their Communication Template tool. It took me about an hour to get the hang of the tool, and I was using it effectively by the end of a single day. What Teresa and Chuck had to say was so simple, so obvious, and yet I had been totally missing it all my life. And not only me, I could look around at other speakers and professional communicators and see immediately that they were also missing the essential insight that almost instantly transforms the way anyone could communicate.

But it didn't stop at just the insight. The great power of what Teresa and Chuck do lies in the Communication Template, and the eight-step thinking process that I now do before every kind of important communication situation in both my business and personal life. I thought it would be good just for speeches. What I have discovered since is that I'm using the twenty-minute thinking process before writing my books, recording audio presentations, writing letters, designing educational processes and before all manner of important meetings, both one-on-one and with groups.

Teresa and Chuck often say that I'm their number one "template addict," and if that's true, I'm proud of the reputation. I would never consider approaching any situation for the rest of my life where it's crucial that I connect with individuals and audiences, without using the template. In other words, it's something that has become totally natural and automatic for me.

I love Teresa and Chuck's approach to communication for three reasons. It's totally non-manipulative, completely humane and leads to a constant growth of confidence. By non-manipulative what I mean is that it doesn't rely on any kind of tricks "to get people to do what you want them to do." By humane I mean that just following their approach and mastering the tool, you become a better human being. Not only that, because of the impact that you make, you also allow other people's humanity to come to the surface. From the standpoint of confidence, I've noticed after using their tool for more than six years that I have this deep, solid sense that I can handle absolutely any kind of communication situation, no matter how high the stakes, no matter how big the audience.

Since The **Power To Connect** philosophy and the Communication Template have worked so well for me, I have continually introduced it into daily situations in my company, and have highly recommended it to hundreds of my clients. We have seen a big jump in the communication effectiveness of the company, and all the clients who have used Teresa and Chuck's approach are reporting similar results.

I took it as a great compliment and also as an excellent opportunity when they asked me to write this foreword. When your teachers ask you to recommend them to their readers, it's a definite recognition of personal progress. Naturally, I used Teresa and Chuck's tool before I started. Writing this to you has given me an opportunity to put into words the profound impact that their innovation has had on my life. I hope that I have connected with you, and that you are now enthusiastic about reading the whole book – as quickly as possible. Teresa and Chuck used their own philosophy and tool to write the book, and simply by reading the book you will grasp the philosophy and learn how to use the tool. It will be the only book that you will ever need to read on this subject.

Dan Sullivan
President and Founder
The Strategic Coach

"Our plans miscarry because they have no aim. When a man does not know what harbor he is making for, no wind is the right wind."

-Seneca

2

Chapter 1

Problems & Power

We're facing a tremendous problem living in the 21st century. The moment when this problem really became clear to us, when it really hit home, was while we were preparing to write this book. We were at an amusement park near our home. It's one of those huge parks with lots of roller coasters, those big death defying, inside out, and upside-down roller coasters. We were there because, for his tenth birthday, our son wanted to go to this park with five of his best friends. In a moment of insanity, we said yes. And so we were at the park with six ten-year-olds. Which, if you think about it, is like herding kittens. Just as soon as you think you've got control of one, another one is wandering off. They're constantly moving, and squirming and going off in all directions. They're all over the place. Ten-year-olds are like this naturally in any situation. But you bring them to an amusement park, a place designed to distract, and it's like herding kittens in a catnip factory. And here we are, trying to communicate with them. We're the responsible adults and have to make sure that we don't lose any of them.

We're saying "Okay, who's your buddy? Make sure you stay together. What time are you supposed to meet up? Does everyone have a watch?" and so on. And what we're competing with, what we're up against here are roller coasters, arcade games, a water park, music, life-sized cartoon characters, they've got their friends, noise, food, and so on. We're talking to boys who want to get to it. And the last thing they want to be doing, the very, absolute, guaranteed last place on earth they want to be is in the parking lot, listening to us talk about logistics and when to come back.

By the time they went off in all directions we were wiped out and not at all sure that what we were trying to say to them was getting through. We talked about what had happened. Right then we realized that this is exactly like all the situations we, as communicators, face everyday when we're trying to communicate something that is very important. It might be something critical to someone's safety and well being, or vital to support someone in doing what they want to do. It could be an important message for a client in your business. You might be telling a potential client about your unique product or service in order to have them buy from you. Or you could be speaking to staff and colleagues to motivate them to take action in your business. Or you could be trying to get your kids to clean their room. We have to communicate. We must get through the distractions.

We may not be competing with roller coasters or cotton candy. And we may not have the attention spans of ten-year-olds to contend with but we are dealing with distractions. We are competing with an unheard-of level of disruption that everyone deals with in this day and age.

This is the problem we're facing in the twenty-first century. We've got vast amounts of information coming at us every day, from every conceivable source and we've got to deal with it. We've got the TV, the Internet, driving down the road we see billboards, hear the radio. We've got books, magazines and newspapers. You walk into your office and there are 17 emails, 9 phone calls and 6 people standing outside your office waiting to talk to you. So we're competing with that.

This information overload, this variety of distraction is something that we are all dealing with. Not only are you dealing with it, but more importantly, so is everyone you are trying to communicate with. So your job as a communicator has gotten more complicated and more challenging, as if you needed any more challenges. Your job as a communicator is to somehow break through that distraction, all that noise that bombards people and deliver your communication. Your job is to navigate through the clutter and really connect with them.

We want to mention a few facts here. Just so we can get a sense of the size of this problem. Recently a computer chip manufacturer announced that they had developed a chip that could house, on one single chip, all the information that had been written down in the history of the world.

– All of it.

– On one chip.

That's pretty amazing. But what's even more amazing is that while doing this research they discovered that the amount of information we have, as a civilization, written down and documented – fully twenty percent of it was created in 1999. That is an extraordinary statistic. We don't have the stats yet for the years following 1999, but we can be sure that the invention of new information certainly didn't slow down since then. In fact we do know that the amount of information is doubling about every three to five years. Which means that by 2020 the amount of info available will be five hundred times that which is available now.

There are tons of these statistics, each one more shocking than the last. You've likely seen the New York Times Sunday edition. It's actually in the Guinness Book of Records as the largest newspaper in the world. But still it's only one newspaper, on one day, for one week in one city. But that newspaper on an average Sunday contains more information than the average person alive in the 18th century saw in their entire lives.

And that is The Problem.

How can we possibly break through that? How can we, when we need to communicate something, possibly get through the barrage of information that assaults those we wish to communicate with, and actually have a conversation with someone? How can we speak to someone who is only saying: "No more! No more! No more!"

That's what this book is about. All our work, our courses, coaching and now this book are dedicated to cutting through that clutter, to helping people like you transform their communication skills, so that they can truly connect through all the noise that we all, in the modern world, are dealing with.

Background/History

The **Power to Connect** is about communication. For more than thirty years we've been helping people create and deliver effective communication. We've created and produced marketing and corporate communication initiatives for Fortune 500 and entrepreneurial clients and produced Emmy-Award winning television programs. We've had the privilege of coaching corporate leaders, entrepreneurs, political candidates, professional speakers, and television personalities to become better, more inspiring, more thoughtful, more powerful, and – most importantly – more effective communicators. Working on professional communication has taught us a lot about human communication in general. What we've learned through our experiences as coaches for some of the most inspiring and effective communicators in the world, as well as being speakers ourselves, is what this book is based on.

The following chapters are designed to have you break through the communication clutter, the information noise that distracts all of us. It's based on our experiences. It is a process we use in designing the marketing and communication strategies and the productions that have had so much impact over the years. It is a process that works in all communication situations, whether it be a sales call, a staff performance review, investment portfolio review with clients. This template will lay the foundation for clearer, more effective communication that yields the results you desire.

To begin with, it is best to use this book in practical application. While the theory in this book is sound and effective, it's in the practice that the real results reside. You will see that there are exercises included in the book to take the thoughts presented here and put them into practice, for that's where the results happen. You may wish to read the entire book first and then go back and complete the exercises or you may wish to do the exercises as you go. Either way will work. The most important thing is to become comfortable in applying the thinking housed here. The template serves as a guide, a structure to open up and access your communication in a way you have not done before.

So let's begin.

The place to start is first to identify the types of communication situations you are in. Most of us may not even realize how often we communicate on a daily basis. In fact, we may not even think of ourselves as communicators except at those times when we give speeches, make presentations. In fact, we are all communicators. That's how we get things done with other people. Unless you're locked in a room by yourself 24 hours a day or live in a cave on the top of a mountain, you are a communicator. And your success as a communicator depends on your ability to get your message through the clutter, the morass of others who want to get their message through the clutter. It's not just the CEOs, the bosses, the managers, and the sales people who are communicators. It's all of us; the moms, the computer service guy, the receptionist, the accountant, the lawyer, the planner, the policeman. All are communicators and the better we are at it, the better the results.

So we're all communicators, but when do we communicate? All the time. It's so second nature to most of us, we don't even think of it as communication. But it's still an exchange of ideas and information to influence or direct someone's opinions or ultimately their actions

The Template

Each of the chapters of this book corresponds to a section of the **Power to Connect** *template we've provided. At the end of each chapter you'll be asked to fill out that section. We've designed the template so that you can see your entire communication organized on a single sheet of paper, so we encourage you to use the template. At each exercise we'll show you the section you should use and how to use it. Scrap paper is a good idea but write your answers down in this book – it's what you have it for. And you can always get more blank templates (the address is at the back of the book).*

THE POWER TO CONNECT® WORKSHEET

Communication situation: ____________________

Date: ____________________

THEM	APPRECIATE
1	1
2	2
3	3
REMEMBER	**OBSTACLES**
1	1
2	2
3	3
FEEL	**VALUE**
1	1
2	2
3	3
DO	**YOU**
1	1
2	2
3	3

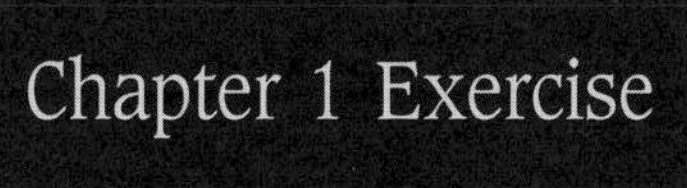

Chapter 1 Exercise

In the space provided list every communication situation you expect to find yourself in over the next week, in all areas of your life, not just business or home.

For example you could write:

- “Speak to my boss about year-end”
- “Review portfolio performance with co-investors”
- “Address colleagues about charity fund-raiser”
- “MC my sister’s wedding”
- “Review sales staff performance and explain changes in the compensation structure”

  and so on

Some examples our clients have listed are:

- Speaking to groups of 500+ sales people to motivate them to sell more
- Regular staff communication to delegate tasks and responsibilities
- Tradeshow sales

These are some of the more challenging situations, much like the amusement park with 10-year-old boys. Lots of noise and distractions to contend with.

- Seminars

These are a popular situation for many in the financial services industry with the challenge to differentiate.

- Letters to prospects

This also constitutes another communication situation and in some regulated industries is subject to compliance review.

- Conversation with the compliance officer

More and more clients say that many of their communication situations are about changes within their organization and the necessary changes in behavior that may be met with resistance.

All of these are business situations. We're all in personal communication situations too:

- Convincing the highway patrol to not give a ticket for speeding.

- Returning a gift without a receipt

- Making travel arrangements for the family vacation
- Conversations about why the dog should not sleep on the couch

While not all of these situations will apply to everyone, the intent is to start recognizing the number and variety of communication situations we're in on a daily basis. Situations in which we have a point of view, have a specific result we'd like to see, and a situation that requires at least one other person's agreement and buy in.

As you start listing all the situations you're in, both in your business and personal life, you may notice that some times you're a more successful communicator than others. By following the process outlined in the template, you will begin to see why and be able to more consciously become more successful, more consistently. And you'll be able to identify what went wrong when it didn't work.

After you've completed the list of situations you expect to find yourself in during the next week, choose one to focus on and work through the process. Now on the worksheet, write down the communication situation you'll be working on and when and where it will take place.

Fill in all your communication situations below.

Communication situations

____

____

____

____

____

____

____

____

Now choose one situation to focus on.

Communication situation: ____________________

____

Date: ________________________________

Chapter 2

Them

We begin laying our foundation for a successful outcome in our communication by first looking at "Them". From this point on, we'll talk about designing your communication for an "audience", what we refer to as "Them". What we mean is the people you'll be communicating with. Sometimes that may be an actual audience, when you're giving a presentation at work, delivering a sermon or a talk at school, etc. or it may simply be a conversation with a colleague or family member, or an email or phone call to one other person. In any case we'll still call them your 'audience', so that we get used to the idea that we're crafting communication with the intention of having someone else hear it. So even if you're using this book to design a conversation with your spouse or kids, think of them as your audience. It will be helpful. Because it forces us to remember that this is not theoretical, but a real conversation with real people we're working on. And it forces us to consider our relationship to those people, and their importance to the communication we're designing.

16 Them

At this point, we should talk about a danger most people face when they start to think about their audience. The danger is *vagueness.* We approach our communication and our audience in generalized terms, and as a result we don't get to be very connected. When you know specifically who you're communicating with you'll be well equipped to actually address their concerns, what's important to them. This leads us to the second most prevalent danger or pitfall when we're communicating: we assume we know to whom we're talking. We say, "Of course I know who they are," without really stopping to think about it. We paint with a broad brush and make assumptions when, in fact, we don't *really* know who they are.

> "Did you ever observe to whom the accidents happen? Chance favors only the prepared mind."
> - *Louis Pasteur*

So we begin then by asking the question "Who am I speaking to?" It seems like a simple, innocuous question. But it is actually a powerful tool for delivering a much more effective communication. We take it for granted most of the time when we're delivering a communication, especially when it's to a single person we know. Because, well, we know them, so of course we *know* them. Or we let ourselves off the hook because we're talking to a roomful of people so how could we possibly know all of them. But both attitudes are dangerous. Because knowing who you're talking to, understanding who they are, what their concerns are, what is important to them is the secret to creating a connection with them.

By knowing who, they are we can get into a relationship with them. You can't connect with people you don't know. You can't answer any of their questions, address their concerns, and provide value for their lives, if you don't know who they are. The first place to start with this question is to write down all the things you know about the people you're speaking to. Start with demographics. How old, what gender, what race, what level of income, what pastimes, interests and hobbies, what do they do for fun, where do they socialize, do they have families, what is their political feeling, are they environmentally concerned, do they drink, do they smoke, do they watch organized sports, do they have younger families, are they worried about social security and old age pensions, are they immigrants, first generation families or have their families always been here and so on.

This information, apart from telling you about the people, will begin to tell you what their concerns are, what it is that these people care about, and what questions they are asking.

Let's take a quick example. Imagine you're a financial planner and your market (and therefore your audience) is business owners with a net worth in excess of $1.5 million. Is that enough information to present to them or pitch them for their business? Probably not. Think about it. What kind of businesses are they running? Are they entrepreneurs or running family firms? How old are they? What is the range of their net worth? $1.5 million is different from $10 million and the concerns of those people will be different too. And so on. It's important to have as much information as you can get your hands on about the people you're communicating with.

Of course when you're speaking to a large group it becomes a more difficult proposition to truly know everyone as an individual. So instead look at the personality of the group. They likely have a way of operating, a certain mindset. Certainly some of them will fall outside of that, but you can get a sense of who the group is. There will be a certain energy about them. There will be a certain approach to life. Are they all men? Are they all women? Half and half? What's the age group? At what stage are they in their careers? Why are they even listening to you speak? What is it about your topic that has them want to hear what you have to say?

There's a strategy we particularly recommend for speaking to large groups of people. If you find yourself giving a talk or presentation to a room, don't just show up and give your talk. Instead begin by mingling with the guests prior to the presentation. Chat to them, join conversations, listen to what they are saying. When you do go to the front of the room to speak, your experience will be different, because you will already be connected with them. You'll know them, at least a little bit.

By knowing who you're talking to, whether it's one individual or 500 conference attendees, you can know their concerns.

By knowing their concerns, you can connect with them. One-size-fits-all doesn't work in communication. There really is no 'too much' in terms of what you can know about your audience. If you were speaking to a roomful of people who, it turns out, were mostly recent immigrants, and you used pop-culture references from the eighties and nineties, you can see how you'd be staring at a sea of blank faces. Your audience wasn't brought up watching MASH or Seinfeld, or listening to Michael Jackson and it's a pretty good guess they would not get many references to these things. By knowing this about your audience you can make your communication more specific to them. And when you do this, your audience knows you made the effort to get to know them, that you had genuine concerns for who they are and what they want.

Chapter 2 Exercises

Exercise One

In the space below write down everything you know about the people you'll be speaking to. As much as you can, regardless of whether you think it relevant to your communication or the topic at hand.

When you've done this examine your results. If you don't know at least 5 different things about your audience then you need to do some research. This may seem extreme but it really will form the basis for the connection between you and your audience. Because to walk into a room and have a conversation with someone knowing nothing about them, just assuming that whatever you have to say will fit them, regardless of who they are or what they need or want, is just trusting the results to fate.

Read over what you've written down about your audience. Now consider this, how much of what you've written is from your own point of view? How much of how you describe them is in relation to you? Probably a lot. Maybe all of it. If you're working on a conversation you want to have with potential clients for your business, did you describe your audience as 'prospects'. We can guarantee you that none of them think of themselves that way. Do you? Would you describe yourself as 'prospective long distance subscriber'? Probably not. If your local phone company relates to you that way, how effective do you think their communication is going to be?

Consider that everything you know about your audience should not be what you think of them but what they think of themselves. Did you describe your audience as 'middle-aged'? Well if you are thirty and your audience is 45 you may see it that way, but ask your average 45 year-old to describe themselves and you'll find few who'll call themselves 'middle-aged'.

So go back and re-create your list, but now get inside the heads of your audience, describe them how they would describe themselves. Because our concerns, interests, objectives and desires are based on how we see ourselves in the world, not on how others perceive us. If our intention is to relate to someone's concerns we should learn more about what that person considers those concerns to be.

Dan Sullivan at The Strategic Coach has created a format for looking at your audience in an especially powerful way, called the D.O.S.™ Worksheet. In this case, D.O.S. stands for Dangers, Opportunities, and Strengths. Using the Strategic Coach D.O.S. model, you identify the dangers or worries and concerns facing your audience from their perspective. This gives you some powerful insights into what they're thinking about and what motivates them to take action.[i]

If you do this thoroughly you'll know as much about your intended audience as is possible without actually knowing them. So what next? Well next is where you actually get to know them. You get into a relationship with your audience.

As we've mentioned before, if you're giving a speech to a large number of people or leading a workshop there are strategies you can use to get to know your audience. But for most of you who are not speaking formally to a big group, this book is about designing much more informal communications. This is good news because you're likely to actually know and be in a relationship with the people you're speaking to. Or you can be on the verge of getting to know them if it's a new relationship. If you're having a conversation with a colleague or two, or are paying a sales call to a potential client you have the chance to know not just about them, but know them specifically. If you know what your potential client's concerns are, what he faces in his business, what his challenges are in terms of his own company, competition and competing suppliers, then you're much more likely to deliver a communication that addresses those needs as opposed to some generic broadcast message that may or may not have something to do with his business.

And this is what forms an effective communication. At any level, whether we're talking to 5000 people or 1, the core idea is the same, if we know who we are speaking to, and therefore know what they want, need, desire, who they are and so on, then the communication we deliver by default, will address those concerns.

Exercise Two

Take the list you have just created and narrow it down to the 3 most important attributes. Fill them in, in the space below.

THEM
1
2
3

Chapter 3

What's in it for me and Why do I care?

When designing and delivering a communication, to one person, or to a thousand, it's important to be connected to our audience. It's essential to effective communication that a strong relationship exist between the speaker and those being spoken to. And it's primarily up to the speaker, not the audience, to establish that relationship because it's the speaker who's choosing to have the communication. That relationship is the core component of how we, as human beings, communicate with each other.

Consider that when someone is speaking to you, in a formal or informal setting, there are a lot of things running through your mind, as you listen and try to decide how much credence you should give the speaker. You may not consciously consider it, but on some level you wonder, "Why should I listen to this person? Why should I give weight to what he says?" and so on. We are judging and evaluating everything, before deciding how to deal with the information being given to us. We ask: "Does the speaker care about me, does he understand me, know what my concerns are, have experience with my problem? What can he show me/tell me/give me that I don't already know? How can he add to my experience of my world in a way that will leave me satisfied?"

This is because at all times, in all communications, the people on the receiving end of the communication are asking themselves two questions. These questions are so important that when we're coaching people we tell them to go to a tattoo parlor and have these two questions tattooed prominently on their bodies, to continually remind them that their audience is always, always asking themselves these questions. Those two questions are:

What's in it for me?

And

Why do I care?

All of us operate as though we are the center of the universe. It doesn't start or stop when we're teenagers. It actually extends all the way through our lives. This is because for our brains, we *are* at the center of the universe. Our brain only experiences the world through our eyes, our ears, our sense of touch, taste and smell. At all times, as we go through life we look at everything around us and we filter it through our brains. The questions our brain uses to filter all the info that is coming in are 'What's all this mean to me and why do I care about this?' Everyone does this. We do it. You do it and everyone you're trying to communicate with is doing it too. So if you, as a communicator, are not keeping that in mind as you are looking at who those people are, you are not going to connect with them. You are not going to be able to communicate to them. You are not going to get the results that you want to get. And you can't answer that central question if you don't know who the Them is. If you don't know, if you're not able to identify Them very clearly, very specifically, you will not be able to answer the questions that your audience is asking. If you're looking at them in very generalized terms it's not going to make any difference. We know that if we want to create effective communication we had better answer those questions, from the perspective of our audience.

These kinds of questions lay at the core of human communication. Our senses are incredible and can absorb tremendous amounts of information constantly; our brains are the most powerful computers on earth, each one scanning, sorting, filtering and making thousands of decisions a second. These questions are some of the criteria we humans have developed to do this sorting. The questions may sound self-centered or self-absorbed, but that is just the job of that part of our brain, to try to understand and make sense of the information coming our way. Now if we know that that is how our brains work, doesn't it make sense to design our communication to work with those filters, not work against them? This is not about designing communication to fool people, just the opposite in fact. It's about answering those questions positively before our audience has even asked them.

In order to do that, you as a communicator need to develop a relationship with your audience. How can you expect to answer the questions that are going through a listener's head if you know nothing about that person? And how can you know anything about that person if you are not relating to them?

This is not a difficult thing to do. It is what we, as human beings, always want to do anyway: develop relatedness and connectedness to each other. That's what we respond to. That's what we want in all situations in our lives. We call it different things in different contexts. Respect, understanding, caring, friendship, and so on, but what it is, what it really comes down to is one person feels some connection to another. As a communicator, you create a connection with your audience that leaves them feeling that on some unspoken level you understand and know them. And that feeling is worth millions. Because it can overcome almost anything else. Not to mention that you will feel the same connection back to your audience. Let's face it we like to have that attention, that connection too.

To see this we only have to think of the last time it didn't happen. Remember back to the last time you were in a situation where someone completely took you for granted. A great example that comes to mind is in dealing with a bureaucracy. Remember when you last had to renew your license, or apply for a permit. How did it feel to try to communicate with someone who didn't know you or care to know you, who wouldn't listen, who would only tell you what they wanted to tell you regardless of whether it was the thing you needed or wanted to hear. Remember the frustration of that moment, of being at the mercy of a person who behaved more like a machine than a human. Think about how this made you feel. Is this the feeling you wish to create in your listeners? If the communication you're designing is a business one, is this how you want to leave your clients or colleagues? If this is a conversation with a loved one you're creating, do you want that person to feel un-cared for by you? Probably not.

We can see simply that at the center of any human communication is that connection; the relationship that the people involved in the communication feel with one another. We call this 'relatedness' and it's this that you want to create as quickly as you can with your audience.

You're reading this book because you are interested in improving your communication. The easiest, quickest and most effective way to improve your personal communication is to make sure, at all times that you are related with your audience. If all you do is create a sense in the minds of your audience, at the end off your communication, that they have been understood, respected and genuinely appreciated then you are 150% ahead of anyone else. And your communication will be more effective.

This relatedness encompasses a couple of things: One is being yourself so that when a relationship is established, it's with a real person – *you* – not someone you're pretending to be. Secondly, the focus must be off of you and on the person you're speaking to. This requires breaking the gravitational pull of how we normally live our lives, where we are the center of the universe. We're not saying that viewing ourselves as the center of the universe is bad. It's normal. It just *is*. But in order to be a great communicator, we have to travel to another universe where everything doesn't revolve around us and our perceptions. We have to travel to our audience's universe. That requires some effort and practice and the recognition that you will probably fall back into your own orbit sometimes. It requires diligence to stay focused on someone else and see things through their eyes; many people give up here and say it's not worth it. However, this is the path to great communication.

Chapter 4

It's not about you

Considering how important it is to create a sense of connection and relatedness to your audience, material and even yourself, there are specific things to do as a speaker to make sure that these things are in place. In the real world there are things to do, which at first will be conscious things you think about doing, but as time goes on you'll do them subconsciously and they'll become second nature to you, that will allow you to create these relationships.

The first step to realizing that it's not about us, is to notice for a second how much we're convinced that it *is* all about us. Here's how we do that.

Consider the following sentence:

They are paying attention to me.

32 It's not about you

What's the most important word in that sentence? If you answered "me" then you're wrong. When we tell this to people we're coaching or who are taking our courses they usually howl with indignation. These people, they say, *want* to hear what I have to say. In some cases they're *paying* to hear it. How could I not be the most important part of that interaction?

Well, the answer is simple. It goes back to the two important questions we mentioned earlier, the ones that we said should be tattooed on the backs of your hands. "What's in it for me?" and "Why should I care?" We as listeners ask ourselves these questions because as human beings we find it impossible to *not* consider ourselves in relationship to the world we exist in. What we mean by this is that every piece of information that your senses perceive gets evaluated by your brain, consciously or subconsciously for its relevance to you, for how it affects you. Does it need more attention or can it be safely ignored and so on. Even when we sleep our bodies are doing this for us. You lay in bed and a car goes by your house, your mind hears it, recognizes it and decides that it's not relevant, and you sleep through it. But at the same time a much quieter sound, say the sound of your child waking, or perhaps an intruder's footstep would have you snap awake instantly.

> What we say is important for in most cases the mouth speaks what the heart is full of.
> – *Jim Beggs*

This filtering system that we all have can really be thought of as a series of questions. The form of the questions may vary. A friend asks you to go to a movie. Immediately you think "Do I want to see that movie, do I want to spend time with that person, do I have time to see that movie, do I have plans already that night" and so on. You're trying to make sense of the request and process it. Most of this kind of filtering takes place in a split second without us realizing it, but it does take place.

What is interesting about all these questions is that they can be boiled down to two: "What's in it for me?" and "Why do I care?" Those are the questions that we as humans are asking ourselves constantly, about everything. Especially about communications we are receiving. So it's vital in delivering communication to bear this in mind. Anyone you're communicating to is asking themselves these questions about your communications, because they're humans and that's what humans do.

You're reading this book because you want to improve your communication skills; therefore you need to consider what your audience will be thinking about your communication while you're delivering it.

Looking back at the sentence we wrote earlier the most important word is THEY. Which is not to say that your words are irrelevant, far from it. But you should consider what you're saying, what you're trying to communicate in the following context: what do I have to say to them, what value am I adding to their lives?

In fact you could re-write that sentence to read:

They are paying attention to me to find out what I have to say that will affect their lives and how it may contribute to them in some way.

It may sound like a lot but it is vital to remember. To check this out we can do a quick exercise. Go have a conversation with someone. Listen to someone speak. If there's no one around, turn on the TV and watch a talk show or a news program. Try and listen, really try and pay attention to what you're hearing and try to NOT think about how it relates to you and your world. You'll likely find it impossible. If you find it easy, it's because you can't even hear yourself asking the questions anymore. But they're there. Consciously or unconsciously you're asking yourself the questions necessary to filter out the information you're receiving. What's in it for me? Why do I care?

Let's go back and consider for a second our role as the *originator* of that communication. If you are trying to communicate something to someone and you know they're asking themselves some form of the questions "What's in it for me?" and "Why do I care?" why would you NOT answer them? Imagine a communication designed to answer the very questions we're likely to ask, one where the speaker has already considered that audiences' concerns, issues and interests and speaks directly to them. Likely it would be one powerful communication – and an effective one.

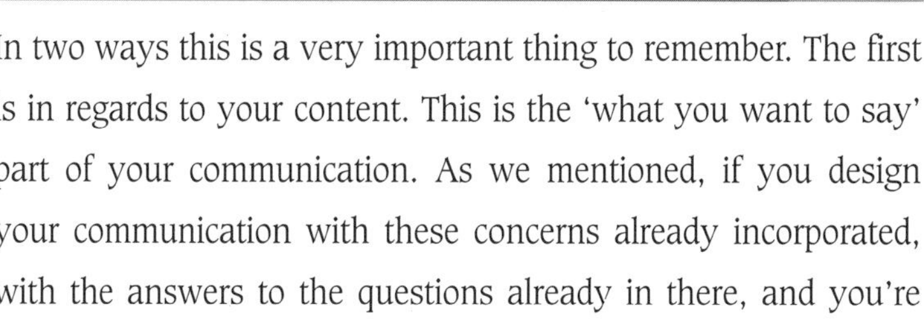

In two ways this is a very important thing to remember. The first is in regards to your content. This is the 'what you want to say' part of your communication. As we mentioned, if you design your communication with these concerns already incorporated, with the answers to the questions already in there, and you're fully focused on your audience, you will deliver value and likely you'll have the experience of a very powerful, effective communication.

In terms of delivery, the actual moment of communication, the most effective, inspiring, moving communication takes place when you are fully focused on your audience. The moment your focus, your attention, strays to yourself and your concerns and your own head, you've lost your connection to your audience. And that is death.

That focus is vitally important. We're talking here about connecting to your audience. That connection cannot take place if you're paying attention primarily to yourself and not to the people to whom you're communicating. You must at all times have your attention out there on them, not on you. This is especially important when we're speaking to someone in person or on the phone. With written communication you have somewhat more opportunity to craft and re-craft your communication before you deliver it. In either case the focus needs to be on those receiving the communication not on you.

This is not always easy to do. We all have, as we've said before, a natural gravitational pull on our attention. That's one of the results of our own filters. Because we're inclined to evaluate information based on its relevance to us, we sometimes get stuck focusing on ourselves exclusively. Now while that can serve us a lot of the time, when we're trying to deliver effective communication it can become an impediment. So it's important to become aware of that gravitational pull and to swing off and break off orbit, so that we can focus on our audience and become aware of their concerns and not obsess about our own.

You'll notice this most often in speaking to someone, not when it's going well, but when it's going badly. Perhaps you're speaking to someone and you see them yawn. It could simply be that they're tired. But we immediately go 'internal'. We start to question: "What's wrong with what I'm saying?" and so on. We question ourselves and the voices in our head start up. You know those voices. The ones that tell us we're not doing a good job, or that we did something wrong. Those voices. And the problem is we start listening to them and reacting to them. And while that's a natural place to go, it's the wrong place to go. Where we're safe, where we're going to be most effective is not in our heads, worried and concerned and doubting, but outside, staying connected to the people we're talking to. This can happen at any time. It's like a little bump in the road and as soon as we hit it, we go internal, focusing on our internal voices and doubts instead of focusing outside and listening to our audience.

How do you know that this is happening? If you find yourself paying attention to what you're doing for a start. Most people start worrying about 'doing' something when they go internal. "What should I do with my hands?" Don't worry about your hands. Your hands know what to do. When you're relaxed, focused on your audience, connected and comfortable, your hands will show up and participate in the conversation. The moment you find yourself worrying about your hands, you should realize that your focus is now on you and red lights and alarm bells should be going off in your head.

At that point you stop, take a moment and get your focus back outside. Re-connect with your audience and remember *it's not about you.*

And about those voices – we all have them. If you can't hear yours it's because they've just melded into the background noise and you've started to believe it's just the sound of your own thoughts. When you're speaking your voices are doing a bunch of different things. They're causing doubt. "What if I lose my place, what if I forget what I was going to say?" and so on. Or they're distracting you "What a nice coat she's wearing, what time is dinner, I must remember the dry cleaning…?" Or they're criticizing you "Oh that wasn't the right word, you're speaking too fast, this was the wrong outfit…?" It goes on and on. These voices are not designed to comfort us or make us feel more confident. So it's not recommended that you pay much attention to them. Instead pay attention to your audience, they're not saying those things to you. The worst they're saying is "Gee, what's this person going to say to me that I can use in my life." And that's a much more interesting question to answer.

Connect to your material

As well as connecting to your audience, which we've seen is the foundation of good communication, you need to connect to your material, to what you're saying to them. What this means is that if there's a reason to say what you're saying (and there should be or what's the point in saying it) then there must be a good reason to hear what you have to say (or write). Connecting to your material means finding that reason.

Of course the information we're communicating is interesting to us. It's our life's work, or at least something we're passionate about. Or something we believe needs to be communicated to this person. But it may not be so interesting to the person we're trying to communicate to, or at least they may not see it that way. For this reason, it's a good idea to look at your material freshly to understand the reasons your audience would want to hear it so that you can have a fresh appreciation for the information yourself.

This does two very important things. It will give you a great insight into the minds of your audience, understanding what they are thinking about what you have to say to them, what their interests are and so on. It reminds you that even though your communication is about your topic, it's about them – their appreciation, understanding and interest in what you're saying. And if you have this in mind you will deliver a communication that speaks directly to the needs, interests and desires of your audience.

The second thing that this does will seem strange to some folks. And for some communications it won't even be relevant. But when you're speaking to people about something that means a lot to you and you consider the interests of your audience and the reasons that someone would want to know what you have to say, it re-invigorates you as regards your subject. You may be communicating something that you've lived, breathed and worked for many years, but going through the process of looking at it from a different perspective will provide a surprising look at your life's work, perhaps in a way that has you fall in love with it all over again.

By "connect with your material", we mean "stop taking it for granted". Look at it again with fresh eyes, re-read it, think about any assumptions you're making, imagine yourself as a listener who knows nothing about it, articulate the reasons that anyone should listen to this material at all. What IS in it for them? Why SHOULD they care?

The point is to have you relate to your material as freshly and strongly as possible. Any communication you deliver, verbal or not, conscious or not, is an honest expression of a genuine sentiment.

One of the most powerful and succinct reasons for connecting with and believing in your material is that if you don't believe what you're saying, what makes you think anyone else will, or should? People can tell when they're being lied to. Recent studies show that the ability to pick out liars is not based in intelligence or training but that as humans we have an instinctual ability to spot liars – even very good ones. And a communicator who doesn't know or trust the material being presented is a liar, plain and simple, and as humans we have a hard-wired, built-in ability to spot them.

Consider how effective we'll be as communicators if we are perceived, even on a subconscious level as being liars.

Chapter 5

Remember

Next we answer the question "What three things do I want my audience to remember?" Narrowing down what we want to communicate is one of the most difficult things to do. One of the reasons we think that we've got to say a whole lot is that we just know a lot, especially those of us who have a lot of experience or are experts in our field. You know a lot of stuff, right? We can hear the objections. "I know way more than three things. Three things are not going to get the result."

The other reason is that there's a perception that *volume* is where the value lies. We think the audience will not get the value unless we take the dump truck and give them all of it. If they don't get everything we've got, know, and experienced, they won't think they got anything. So it's out of that fear and desire to create value that we give too much information.

Remember at the beginning of the book, we talked about The Problem? All the information we're all faced with and need to process? Guess what. Nobody can remember more than 3 things. Sometimes, we can't remember one thing! And communicators add to the problem by approaching what they're trying to convey by telling you everything they know about their topic. The approach is "Here's everything I know about this. Here you go. I'm going to dump it on you. Now, can you make a decision?" And your audience can't make a decision. They become immobilized by all the information. They feel buried with too much. Their natural filtering system is going to kick in and they will narrow all your information to the three things they can remember, or worse they'll throw it all out as useless because they can't be bothered filtering.

Since you're the one trying to get results, why don't you identify the most important points you want to get across, rather than leave it up to chance? Pick the three that will support the results you are looking for and leave them with that.

People don't hire ad agencies and tell them to just do whatever they feel like. Do you think Pepsi would just call up their ad agency and say "Oh gosh, I don't know, why don't you just make an ad for us saying whatever you like. Oh, anything at all is fine, really." Of course not. Pepsi, like every other successful company is keenly aware that their message – what companies call a 'brand' – is incredibly valuable and that just saying any old thing will weaken it and eventually no one will know what 'Pepsi' means anymore. So why should your communication – call it your own personal brand – be any different? It shouldn't.

We're interested in designing clear focused messages that deliver the results we want. We don't lob ideas and facts out randomly and hope that some audience somewhere picks up on enough of them – enough of the right ones – to get us some result we may want.

And by results remember we mean whatever you have decided is important out of this communication. So back to the example at the beginning of the book, 6 ten-year-olds back at the car safe and sound was what we were after.

Of course, it can be less than three. It can be one thing that you want people to remember. When you start inching your way up to more than three, catch yourself. When you find yourself saying, "I've got three, but I'm just going to add this fourth one in. It's just a little one." And then you say, "Well, I got away with that fourth. I'm just going to add that fifth one in." And the next thing you know, you're back up to a list of ten things you want them to remember and your audience is gone. They're not paying any attention.

Chapter 5 Exercises

Exercise One

Recognizing that you know a lot, you're now going to brainstorm. What are all the things that you want them to remember? Start listing all the stuff in that communication situation that you want people to remember. This is so you can get it all out of your head. Don't edit at this point. Just let it all get down on paper. You may find writing it as bullet points gives you enough. You may find writing it all out helps. Do what works best. The intent is to get all the information out so you can make decisions about how you want to handle it, make decisions about what is essential and what is ballast. Here's your opportunity to brain dump, vent, get it all out. Write down everything you want them to remember in this specific communication situation. Some of the examples of what you might include here are:

- How you normally approach the situation your audience is in
- How long you've been in business
- This is how you work
- By going into this joint venture with us, you will make lots of money

- I can bring you "A" clients
- We have a way to make you wealthy
- Because of a shift in the business climate, we are changing our business model
- We have a great plan to implement the changes that will bring greater opportunity to all the staff

Now remember, we didn't ask you to write down everything you're going to say to them, this is not a meant to be a list of every story, anecdote, statistic or illustration that you'll share with them in the course of a 5 minute phone call or 2 hour meeting. We're talking simply about the things you expect, or hope they will recall later about your conversation or speech or meeting.

What I want them to remember.

____

____

____

____

____

____

____

____

____

____

Exercise Two

Now, narrow down the brainstorming list you just completed to just three things. As you're evaluating which three things you want to include, now is an appropriate time to test against those two questions, 'What's in it for me?' and 'Why do I care?' When you're looking at the three things that you want people to remember and if it's not answering those two questions either re-word it so that it does, or get it off the list. Take a look at your own experiences. The things that you remember are the things that are relevant to you. It's the same with everybody else. If what you want them to remember isn't relevant, clearly stated in terms that they can understand how it applies to them, it's not going to make it through the filter.

- Look at all those things that you wrote down that you'd like your audience to remember, narrow it down to just three things.
- Then, evaluate if it answers for them, 'What's in it for me?' and 'Why do I care?'
- If it doesn't, get rid of it.

REMEMBER

1
2
3

48 Remember

Do you have, on your list, that you want your audience to remember that you've been in business for thirty-five years? This is one we see commonly when we're doing workshops with clients. And what we say is, why do they need to know that? What is in it for them? If you can't answer those questions about a particular point then cross it out.

Maybe that's a supporting fact, a detail, or part of an anecdote. You may establish that you've got some experience, that you're not making this up as you go. But that's a supporting argument. There's a big difference between this information, and saying "We can help you retire a millionaire", which is obviously a much more relevant, compelling piece of information for a potential client to take away.

What we're getting to here is the *worst-case scenario* information. If this person were only going to remember three things, and absolutely nothing more, what would you have them be? What three things are essential?

We haven't chosen the number three arbitrarily, there's a lot of reasoning behind that. To begin with three is a good number to play with. Too many more and people start to lose the thread, or details or the connections between things. Less than that is not making good use of their memory. Three works well in that, apart from being a nice easy group and size to remember, they work well logically in our minds. We can have someone remember that because of A, B happens and therefore C is the answer. Or A and B are current conditions and C is the future we seek.

For example,

A person in financial services wants to form an alliance with a CPA firm. He writes down the following:

A) CPAs are facing increasing competition and commoditization

B) The CPA relationship with their clients presents unique opportunities

C) Our firm has a program that supports CPAs in reducing the impact of commoditization and competition and capitalizing on their unique opportunities

Now if the people he's speaking to at the CPA firm remember only three things after their conversation, he would like them to be these three things. Because the natural consequence to knowing these three things is that you would look at going into partnership with this person. Right?

Conceptual vs. Concrete

Another obstacle to be aware of as you're honing your three key things to remember is, as communicators, one of the reasons our communication doesn't get through is that we think conceptually and we communicate conceptually. The problem is that is not how people understand. For example, a participant in our **Power to Connect** workshop is a financial advisor, working with high net worth individuals. His communication was to be delivered to bankers, persuading them to form a strategic partnership in which both would make introductions to their best clients. He stated that one of his three things was that he "would have the bank's best interests in mind". We probed what that meant, to "have their best interests in mind"? Because his audience was going to have to translate what that meant. In fact, he meant that he would be making recommendations based on what would benefit the bank's clients, not what would benefit him. Stated in that way, the translation from what he was saying into specifically "What's in it for me?" was accomplished.

If, when you identify the three things you want the audience to remember they have to do a translation, they may decide it's not worth the effort. It's more work than they're willing to put into it. Mentally, if not physically, they'll leave. Your audience may even say, "Okay this is what you want me to remember but I don't understand what you mean by 'you have my best interests in mind.'" They have to do the translation to answer what's in it for them. They have to work to accept what you are proposing. Some people will do that work, do the translation, but most people won't. For the ones unwilling to translate, the response is "I don't get it, I'm out of here."

The next translation we ask our audience to make is how what we're saying is relevant in their lives, or 'Why do I care?' Back to our example of the financial advisor, after he went from stating one of his three things as having their best interests in mind to making recommendations focused on what would benefit the bank's clients rather than being driven by what would benefit him, he still needed to let them know why that was important. It was important because they had an unstated concern about risking the bank's reputation by exposing their best clients to someone else's advice. It may seem unnecessary to state the obvious here for the client, to state why they care that this advisor would put the bank's clients concerns before his own. You may think that they would just know. It may seem obvious to some why that is important, yet it is those assumptions that leave our audiences with more work to do to understand what we want them to understand. Remember they don't *have to* hear anything you have to say. *It's up to us to make clear what we want to communicate. It's not up to them to understand!*

The point is, we speak conceptually and require our audiences, the ones we hope to influence, the people we are dependent on for results, to make the translation from the conceptual to 'how does that apply to me.' When we do the translation for them, our audience is left saying "Oh that's interesting. I understand what you're saying. It's important for me to do this particular thing because it impacts me in this way."

Trust your audience to make the leap from what you're talking about into their own lives. We want to speak conceptually because we are afraid of saying something specific in case it's not literally what the audience is thinking. So we stay so vague and up in the air that we're not clear about what we are saying. Trust your audience to make the connections to their own lives. They'll do this most effectively when you are specific.

Another example comes from our client, Steve. His first point was that he wanted his audience to remember that there's real value in going through his unique business process. To begin with, we suggested that saying "There's real value in the unique process" is conceptual. It's conceptual because it relies on his audience to translate 'real value' into something concrete that's in it for them. If they're not inclined, or in the mood, that's the end of the communication. We asked Steve what the real value is. He replied that the process identifies, eliminates, and protects them from financial pitfalls, some of which they're not even aware of.

Now his audience may say, "I get that there's value there for someone, but why do *I* care about that?" So Steve will have to do a second translation that tells his audience why they need to know what those pitfalls are. It is as if he were first saying, there are some potholes on the road ahead and if you hit one, it will break the axel on your car and that will cost you a bundle of money. Now that's something that his audience can get their head around. That's a specific point that you can understand and immediately see whether or not it applies to you.

Steve's second point was that his unique business process will lead to increased wealth. Now that has my attention. I can easily answer "What's in it for me?" and "Why do I care?" As someone in the audience, I'm interested in hearing more.

His third point was that 'he knows what he's doing and knows how to get the audience to increased wealth.' Up to now (with the suggested changes we've made) the audience is with you.

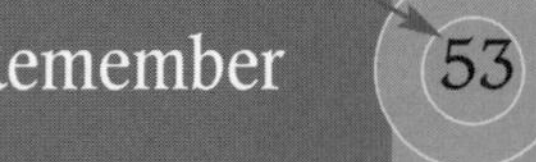

Then, the attention is shifted back to Steve. As soon as you take the attention off your audience, they're not as interested. Steve shifted it over to himself and in the audience they're saying, "Yeah. Maybe that's true about you, but what about me?"

Let's make an important point here. We're not saying that in your communication, you don't establish credibility. We're simply suggesting that it is possible to establish credibility within the key things that you want people to walk away with. That it can be inherent and doesn't have to be one of the three key things. We've found telling people that you're the person for the job usually raises more questions than it gives a sense of security. It's better demonstrated. In our example with Steve, he has shown that he's got a process that's going to uncover those pitfalls. The process is going to show them how to extend their wealth. So for his last point he could demonstrate, with examples of others who have faced similar situations, how he understands and can provide powerful solutions that work.

It's important to understand that your audience is coming to this communication from a completely different place than you. Unless you meet them, unless you jump over the fence, hang out with them where they are, there is no communication. Or if communication happens, it happens entirely by chance. It really does. And that's why the translation is critical for each of us as communicators. Most of the time, we don't do that. This doesn't mean you've done anything wrong or bad. It is just the nature of the beast. It's the gravitational pull for us as human beings. The more you can break through that, the more you're going to actually be able to impact your results. What we're suggesting to you is by shifting your point of view, all those circumstances where you're not getting the results you want are now available to you in a way that they weren't before. Here's a caution. You will still fall into those same habits of having the attention on yourself. Everybody does. We are the center of our universe. Everything revolves around us. That's not going to stop. It's when you break through, escape that gravitational pull, that you're going to see some different results. That's what this worksheet is all about. It's a way, a process, for you to break away from that gravitational pull so you can start viewing things differently and get better results.

This communication template is a simple way for you to break through all of the noise and the clutter out there in communication. It's a simple easy way of getting your mind straight. Secondly, this applies to all your communication. It's not just for presentations. It's not just for books. It's not just for phone calls. It's for all communication situations. The intent is for you to feel confident as a communicator. It's a way for you to clear yourself going into any communication situation so you get optimal results. That's what's in it for you and why you should care.

Chapter 6

Feel

How will my audience feel after listening to me? To most people this question seems a bit odd. We tend to look at our communication in terms of hard facts. Things we want people to remember, things we want to get across, things we want to achieve, numbers, dates, times, facts. But whether we like it or not we are actually creating an emotional environment when we speak. We are 'generating' for lack of a better word, a feeling in our audience as they listen to us or read our communication. And again as with the earlier parts of the worksheet we've talked about, since your audience will be feeling something *anyway* wouldn't it make sense for you to have a hand in consciously deciding what they'll feel after hearing you?

It's been said, and it's completely true, that people make decisions based on emotion, then use facts to justify what they've decided. If you've bought a car or a house in your life then you know what we're talking about. How many of us have had the experience of walking into a house and feeling that 'this is it' that this is our new home? Maybe it wasn't the ideal house, there were some imperfections, but something told us, something we couldn't put our finger on, that this was 'it'. And we likely spent the next while building a case for it, 'Well the schools are very good around here' and 'It's got great highway access'. This is what we're talking about. Yet in communication design we usually don't think about this response. We think of the 'remember' stuff but not the 'feel' stuff. And as we've said time and again in this book and in the coaching and classes we teach, any time you are not thinking about an aspect of your communication, you are leaving it up to chance – with predictable results.

There is a woman we coach from Houston named Carol Porter. Carol has a great story. She discovered that there are a lot of starving children in Houston. So she created a program like Meals on Wheels, called Kidcare to feed these kids. She was preparing all these meals for the kids in her own kitchen and delivering them with her husband and children out of the back of her car. The city council of Houston, in their wisdom, decided to shut her down – because she didn't have a mop sink in her kitchen and she didn't have a grease hood over her stove! Mind you, she didn't fry anything. And she cleaned her mops in bleach and water that was so hot, she could cook an egg in it. She even demonstrated this to the city council. And the city of Houston told her they were going to shut her down and put her in jail.

When I first started coaching her, she was preparing to speak at the Million Dollar Round Table, to a group of 6,000 of the top insurance agents and financial advisors in the world. The story was very compelling, yet it was missing the emotion. We took her into a room and said, "Carol, you need some righteous indignation in here. You want your audience disturbed. These people, who are motivated, gifted professionals, need to understand that right around the corner from their offices and million dollar homes there are children who are malnourished – children the city council is preventing you from helping." So Carol adjusted her communication, just slightly, so that she was more emotionally connected with her audience. So that they could see some of her indignation, anger, frustration and ultimately her need to help. She became a passionate advocate for children. She argued, not *against* city council, but *for* children to have a good meal. As a result, some pretty successful people started to contribute to her efforts and Carol was able to help more children lead better lives.

By consciously thinking about the environment you wish to create and writing it down, you have a better chance of getting the emotional response to your message that you desire. And the emotional response will help produce the outcome, or results that you set out to achieve. Remember that this is the reason you're communicating in the first place. So be sure when you identify an emotional experience for your audience you choose one that will be likely to produce the results you want. Obviously Carol wanted outrage, anger, concern. These were the kind and strength of emotions it would take to get people to do what she wanted them to do, what she felt passionately needed to be done. Mild anxiety wasn't going to cut it. Vague concern wasn't going to save any children. So think about how you want to leave your audience. Be aware also, as you are identifying what you want your audience to feel, that you actually aren't identifying thoughts. We are, as human beings, more practiced in identifying thoughts than feelings. Look at what the emotions are. They can feel inspired. They can feel excited. They can feel upset or distressed. They can feel confident. They can feel happy. They can feel sad. They can feel any of a full range of emotions. There's not a right or wrong emotion you want them to feel. Just be clear that what you're doing in your communication is creating an emotional experience and identify the type of emotional experience you want to create.

Some examples:

- Appreciated for the work they've done
- Confident about the future
- Disturbed by the consequences of inaction
- Excited about a new opportunity
- Trust in me as an advisor
- Relief at having found a solution
- Inspired to participate

Chapter 6 Exercise

Exercise One

On your worksheet write down the three things you want your audience to feel once they've received your communication. Remember these are not things you want them to *think* but what you want them to feel. If you have more than three, write them all down and then pick the most important ones.

FEEL
1
2
3

Notes about this exercise:

When you identify who you're communicating with, what you want them to remember, and how you want your them to feel, you have a way of evaluating your content, what it is you actually say and the tone. This is the ground work. This is setting your foundation so you can go and develop what's actually going to come out of your mouth or be written on the page or go on the web site. You've created a target for yourself to hit. You know what they look like and are concerned with. You know what you want them to remember. And now you know how you want them to feel. Now you can look at your content, your message and measure it against those criteria.

If you want somebody to feel excited, guess what? You need to create some exciting content. You're not going to be able to have boring content and have people feel excited. It simply doesn't work. Use the work you're doing here as your way of measuring the content you create. Is it for this audience? Is it all about them? Is it answering the questions for them, *what's in it for me* and *why do I care*? Does it emphasize and reinforce the things you want them to remember? Does it start eliciting the kinds of emotions you desire? And if it doesn't, you need to go back and re-look at those things written up to now or you need to recreate your content so it matches your strategy up to this point. By doing this, you have a way to operate very, very specifically.

This part can be hard to do. We've often written things, or talked about things a certain way and we're comfortable with them, and now we find that they don't really support our communications objectives and we're faced with a dilemma, do we keep it or kill it? We were working with a client who had created a presentation to potential clients. During our work with him he realized that an elaborate metaphor he had created to talk about the changing cost of consumer items over time simply didn't work. It was complex, multi-layered and ultimately confusing for his listeners (it was a live speech he was working on). But the client loved this metaphor – he didn't want to let it go. And finally after trying for hours to shoe-horn this metaphor into his presentation, he realized that it was too confusing for people – they couldn't figure out what he wanted them to remember, and it left people a bit concerned, and mostly bored – which needless to say were not the emotional reactions he was going for.

If this is a brand-new communication you probably won't have to worry about this too much, but if you are working on a conversation you've had before and will have again, you may have to be a bit cruel at this point.

If you already have a draft of your communication, review it. If you have notes or an outline review that. What you're looking for here are the answers to the questions we've already discussed. From the perspective of the people you've identified (the THEM) does it answer the questions "What's in it for me?" and "Why do I care?" Are you clear, when looking at what you've got, that you are trying to communicate three things to your audience? And finally, does what you're going to say have the emotional impact that you've decided it should? If you want excitement is your communication exciting? If you've decided 'sad' is it sad? The cruelty comes in here in what you have to do next.

If the answer is no – to any of these questions - if something about your communication doesn't fulfil the criteria then remove it. It may be the funniest anecdote or the most carefully constructed metaphor but if it doesn't contribute then it's not helping. There are no passengers in this – if it isn't rowing, then throw it overboard.

Chapter 7

Do

At this point it's time to identify what you want your audience to do when they receive your communication. Again we're faced with one of those seemingly self-explanatory things which is much more complex the more you look at it. People often say that of course they know what they want their audience to do. They want them to buy something! But really how specific are they being? We like to phrase this as 'Who will do what by when?" That's how specific we want you to be when designing what you want your audience to do.

There was a public service announcement on television recently regarding a rainforest in Belize. A logging company had gone down there and was logging out this particular rain forest to devastating effect. An international conservation group created an announcement with a very famous actor talking about this situation, explaining the devastation happening to the local environment and all the implications economically. It was very moving and we were motivated by it. It left us completely in agreement, feeling very indignant about the whole thing. It was very good at creating an emotional impact. It left us wanting to do something. But here's the kicker: they didn't ask us to *do* anything. They didn't even give us an address to write to or phone number to call. So we were left with no action to take on this issue, no letter to write a congressman, no email to send to the head of this company, no check to send to a cause, no boycott of a product, nothing! As a result that's precisely what we did: Nothing. Not because we lacked motivation, but because we lacked instruction, and that instruction is called the 'Call to Action'.

And that's what happens to communicators. You motivate your audience. You communicate eloquently. You say all of the right things and then you forget to tell them what they're supposed to do next. You just assume that they'll not only see what's possible to do next but how they should do it and so on. And again that's a tremendous amount to leave to chance. Which is why, if you do this one thing, you're going to see a dramatic shift in the results you're getting.

In some cases, there is a call to action, but it's vague or incomplete. For example, a participant in our **Power to Connect** workshop wrote down that he wanted his audience to give him a referral by January 1. We asked him to consider this: "Do they know what they are supposed to do in order fulfill that commitment?" He had given his result as an expression of what his audience would do, but had not called them to action in a specific enough way that they could do it. So as a call to action it was vague and not specific. It would be better expressed as "Over the next two weeks have a look at your client base and highlight any that fit this profile. Then send those contacts to me by the end of that week."

What happens if it's not specific? It doesn't get done. Anyone with kids knows that 'Take out the garbage' doesn't fly, but 'Take out the garbage before dinner or you're not watching TV tonight' carries a bit more weight. And it's not just the threat. The kids respond to the specificity of it, they can understand it and work with that. Whether it's the kids or the clients passing on referrals, if there's no deadline, if it's not specific, we procrastinate. We get into "I'll get to it later" mode. You should recognize that people will always procrastinate unless they get a deadline. They can always choose to decline that deadline, choose another one, or just ignore it. But at least you have them engaged in thinking about 'by when' which means they've likely already accepted the 'who will do what' part.

A word of warning here, be careful of writing the ultimate action you want them to take, which may not necessarily be the *next* step. Actions don't have to be big, monumental steps. By setting the jumps too high and making the "commitment" price tag too great, you can set defeat in motion. Most of the progress you make in communication will occur with a series of small steps and few large leaps. All of the results begin at the beginning, with the first small steps. For example, you want them to attend the winter conference, but the first action they need to take is to register and pay a deposit. Or you may say that the action that you want them to take is to place all their assets under your management. If someone has just met you, they may not be ready to do that. The next action for them may be to provide some information about their situation for you to determine how you can support their objectives. Look to see what the next appropriate step is and keep the momentum going.

Let's take an exaggerated example, just to prove our point. Imagine you've just met someone and you're smitten, in fact you think it's love at first sight. Well, great, but if you ask this person to marry you while standing in line at the bank, you probably won't get very far. So you suggest a coffee together. Your ultimate aim may be to get married, but it is not the logical next step, and therefore shouldn't be your call to action at the end of that communication.

Chapter 7 Exercise

Write down the three things you want your audience to do next. If it helps you gain clarity, start from the broad and narrow it down. Start with the ultimate final step and work back to find out what your audience should do next, right now, today, to have you achieve the results you are working for.

For example:

- Ultimately you want 10 new clients, but you know that you need to make contact with some people first, so your next step could be "Respond to this email by clicking through to our web site and filling out a survey."
- You want to get people involved in your charity, but your next step is "Before you leave put your name and contact information on a sign-up sheet to attend a volunteer orientation."

- You want to be the primary financial advisor for a high net-worth individual at your sales seminar. But your next step is to schedule a meeting in the next week to review their needs.

Fill in the 3 actions you want them to take.

Chapter 8

Appreciate

We've now gotten to one of the most difficult chapters of our book. We've tried to keep everything concrete and avoid the conceptual, but one of the most important aspects of this work, of the ability to design effective communication takes place in the form of a question that most of us have a hard time getting our heads around.

"What do I appreciate about my audience?" Or put another way, what are the things about those people I'm communicating to that make me glad for the opportunity to be here happy to deliver the communication?

We'll examine why we even need to ask this question shortly. First we a have warning to deliver. *This is not about you!* If your first instinct is to write:

- They like me

- They appreciate and value my contribution

- They can make me a lot of money
- They make me happy

Then your attention is in the wrong place. Me-me-me keeps showing up here and you'll realize that all of those sentences are about me, not about THEM. This is not about you at all, it's about them. It means you keep breaking that gravitational pull around your universe and make it about them.

A young woman we work with was using our worksheet to prepare her wedding speech. Initially, she wrote the things she appreciates about her fiancée are:

- He loves me
- Treats me well
- He makes me laugh
- He supports me and is affectionate.

It came as a shock when she realized everything she appreciated about her fiancée was about her. She re-wrote her speech so that she was able to quickly shift the attention away from herself and have her appreciation be entirely about him.

- He's funny
- He's sexy
- He's affectionate
- He's caring, and kind-hearted

In this way her communication to her fiancée was much more meaningful not only to him, but to herself as well.

> "The measure of mental health is the disposition to find good everywhere"
> – *Ralph Waldo Emerson*

Now why is it important to list the things you appreciate about your audience? Are you going to tell them this? You may or may not. You can decide if you're actually going to express it. But it's important to remember something about how we as humans communicate with each other. Every thought, emotion, belief and feeling about your audience, whether you tell them or not, acts as a filter through which you are delivering that communication. If you are thinking only about what they do wrong, what their errors and deficiencies are, what makes them stupid, that will color your communication. That will show up when you are communicating to them.

If, on the other hand, you are holding in your mind all those things you appreciate then *that* is what will filter all you have to say. This all sounds very conceptual and hard to pin down. But we've found that most people know what this is like. We've all been in situations where either we were thinking "Gosh this person is stupid", or some other negative thought and somehow that conversation or presentation didn't go well. Or worse yet, we were the target of some communication that we felt didn't work for us because there was something about the speaker that seemed false or 'off' like he didn't 'get' us. We know how rotten that feels, and how effective that communication was.

This whole question actually came to us when we were driving to present a proposal to a potential client. And we anticipated they were going to be difficult. As we were driving, we were complaining, saying things like, "They're really cheap. They don't really get the level of expertise we're bringing here. They are going to nickel and dime us. There's this wrong and that wrong" until we worked ourselves into a state of upset. We realized we were going down this tunnel of negative communication because of our mindset. And walking in the room with all those thoughts around us like a toxic cloud, there was just NO WAY that the meeting could go well. It would be doomed from the start. So we stopped and said, "All of that may be true, but what is it that we appreciate about them?" We then identified the things we genuinely appreciated about this client. "They have a commitment to creating something of high quality. They have to manage budgets and have a lot of responsibilities, they're very conscientious about..." After we went through this process, it shifted our frame of reference. We went into the situation and started talking to them from a place of appreciation rather than "They're too cheap." If where you're coming from is out of that appreciation, that gets communicated, even if the words aren't said.

Some of you may be in a situation where you have to communicate with people where you really have to dig pretty deeply to figure out what you can appreciate about them. You know there are those kinds of folks in the world. Right? And sometimes, it may be that all you can really appreciate about them is that they're someone's son or daughter, that here are people out there who actually do love them. Or that they take a bath in the morning! You might have to dig. Keep digging to get to that point where you can come from a place of appreciation. And often, what happens, when you come from a place of appreciation, people change miraculously and become easier to appreciate. And someone who is easier to appreciate, is easier to know, and that person is easier to relate to and connect with. And as we keep saying, this is about connecting with your audience. This book is not called "the power to talk to" it's The **Power To Connect**.

Just to get you started, here are some examples of things to appreciate:

- They're hard working
- They have a strong commitment to their family and loved ones
- They're innovative
- They're smart
- They've done a good job protecting their finances
- They're fun to be with
- They make good decisions
- They're persistent
- They're clever
- They're well-dressed

- They have a lot of money
- They are good business-people
- They have nice kids
- They are loving

Notice that none of these examples have anything to do with the communicator. The attention is on the right person, the audience.

Chapter 8 Exercise

Begin this exercise by writing out all the complaints you have about your audience. Don't be afraid to say all those deep hidden thoughts and beliefs, no matter how embarrassing or petty they seem. Just because you don't say them or ignore them, doesn't mean they don't impact your communication. By letting them come to the surface, acknowledging them, you'll be able to substitute them with more powerful thoughts and beliefs.

To begin this exercise, answer the following questions with the first thoughts that come to mind:

Complete the following list of questions to surface any negative thoughts or beliefs about your audience.

1. The thing that really drives me nuts about ___________ (Name of your audience) is ________________________.

2. I don't think this will be a satisfactory relationship with ________________________ (Name of your audience) because of____________________________.

3. My audience really thinks _________________ about me.

4. ________________ just really doesn't get my business because of___________________.

5. This person never listens/listens but ignores me/doesn't understand/doesn't care (circle one)

6. They are only having a meeting with me because of ____________________, not because they want to do business with us.

Now, complete the following questions to find a place of appreciation.

1. ____________________ (Name of your audience) is cared about by their friends and family because of ____________________.

2. ____________________ (Name of your audience) is respected by others because of____________________.

3. ____________________ (Name of your audience) makes a contribution by____________________.

4. ____________________ (Name of your audience) best characteristic is ____________________________.

5. ____________________ (Name of your audience) gets results by ______________________.

6. ____________________ (Name of your audience) will best be remembered for ____________________.

7.________________ (Name of your audience) find the most enjoyment in life because of their ability to __________.

8. The best thing you can say about______________ (Name of your audience) is ______________.

9.________________ (Name of your audience) Unique Ability™ is __________.

10.________________ (Name of your audience) can be counted on for ________________.

Drawing from this list, fill in the three things you appreciate about you're audience.

APPRECIATE
1
2
3

™ Unique Ability is a trademark of The Strategic Coach.

Chapter 9

Obstacles

Okay. We got through the most 'intellectual' chapter, that is, the one that takes place mostly in our heads. Now we will cover some things that are much more real and concrete – Obstacles.

In any communication situation, there are obstacles. We never get a clear channel for our communication. There are things that will get in the way of you getting your message across. Some of those things you will be able to control. Some you won't. What we'll be doing in this chapter is identifying those things that are blocking or clogging the communication channels, those things that are creating static in the line. Obstacles fall into two different categories: environmental and attitudinal.

Environmental Obstacles

Environmental obstacles are things like technical problems and logistical mishaps. With more and more of our communication dependent on technology, sooner or later there will be a technical failure and that will create a communication obstacle, something that will have an impact on the quality of your communication. It may be that your computer doesn't work as you had planned, or your PowerPoint won't link properly to the projector system. It could be that your marketing or workshop materials don't arrive on time. If you've ever given presentations in a hotel, you're familiar with the noise that seeps through the air wall separating meeting rooms. One the most heart-breaking examples of an environment doing everything it could to spoil a communication was told to us by a coaching client. He was giving a morning seminar regarding investment trends and investment advice. As he began his presentation, a marching band began performing in the room on the other side of the air wall. Yes let's just pause there for a second, *a marching band*!!. So you think your day is starting off badly, well at least you don't have to compete with a marching band.

He investigated the cause and discovered there was a national marching band competition in the next room and it was going to last the whole day. Now this client has learned to laugh at the experience, but at that moment he was faced with a tremendous barrier to his effective communication. This obstacle was so obvious, no one could pretend it didn't exist. He had to address it. Since the bands were not going to stop playing, he chose to change the serious tone of his seminar. He decided to have some fun with it and used humor to lessen the negative impact. It wasn't a perfect day, but he managed to make it work.

Some other common obstacles facing communicators are the distracting movement and noise by the wait staff during luncheon (or breakfast or dinner) presentations. Rooms can have posts or other obstructions that block the audience's sight line, windows with views of distracting activities or scenery, lighting that is too dark or too bright.

Chapter 9 Exercises

Exercise One

To prepare as well as you can for your communication situation, do following exercises. Prepare this list now and add any that are appropriate to your own chosen communication situation.

- Create a checklist for your communication situation, especially if it's for a presentation
- Do a site survey of the room where you'll be speaking
- Notice any obstructions that will block the communication
- Complete full technical check with your PowerPoint, audio visual, computer
- Find out what events will be in close proximity to you
- Is any construction or fire drills scheduled during your communication
- Ensure you know how to operate any equipment
- Confirm you have all your support materials and that they are complete
- Know who to contact when something goes wrong

Your number one choice is, obviously, to avoid the obstacles that you may face. A number of the items on the checklist are about making sure you avoid the obstacles or accommodate them when you are trying to communicate. But remember there is always the chance that something will go wrong. And you'll have to deal with that. The secret, if there is one, is in having done the homework for your communication. If you know what you want to say, who you're speaking to, what you want them to remember, feel and do, and so on, then when your projector dies, or the overhead fan is too loud, then the *only* thing you'll be dealing with at that moment is that issue. You won't be trying to figure all those things out at the same time. We've found that when you take care of everything you can anticipate, then the surprises are much easier to handle.

Attitude Obstacles

There is another type of obstacle that is created by preconceived attitudes. All of us as audience members go into a communication situation with our beliefs and thoughts. A very popular one is skepticism. You can see the audience with this arms-crossed look of "Show me" and "I've heard this before" expression on their faces. Clearly, this audience doesn't have an unobstructed channel for communication!

We are all faced, in every communication situation, with the attitudes, beliefs, prejudices that our audience comes with.

As communicators, we never get a clean channel for communication. Think of it this way. When we say you're going to hear a presentation from a CPA, do you have an immediate thought or belief about how exciting the talk will be? Do you experience any cynicism when we suggest a book by an attorney on integrity and trust? What's your first thought about a recommendation to meet with a financial advisor who will show you how to increase your wealth with minimal risk? Do you have a reaction to a suggestion to attend a meeting to hear about a new business opportunity you can do in your spare time, out of your home?

Did you find that you had some immediate preconceived attitudes and beliefs, just by hearing the subject of communication and who would be delivering it? Most of us do. That's why it's important to recognize that you as the communicator are also facing an audience just like you. Before going into the situation, you want to be aware of those attitudes. After that, you can determine how you want to deal with it, or if you prefer you can ignore them. But at least you're not pretending they don't exist.

Exercise Two

List all the preconceived attitudes, beliefs and prejudices that the audience may have that are blocking the channel for communication.

Examples:

- I already do or know this
- I don't have the time
- This will slow me down
- I don't trust (lawyers, insurance sales people, salespeople…)
- I don't have enough money (time, education…)
- My other advisors disagree
- I'd rather be at home watching TV
- I have too much to do already
- I don't want to change

____

____

____

By thinking ahead and acknowledging the obstacles you could be facing, you can create your communication to overcome those obstacles. You can make a choice about whether to actively acknowledge the obstacle or not. Our personal preference is to deal with obstacles directly. If there's a rhinoceros head on the table, say there's a rhinoceros head on the table and don't talk around it. Because we promise that your entire audience will be staring at the rhino head and not at you. But you get to choose. You may feel that you say enough in your communication that any prejudices your audience has will be dealt with. Or you may feel that its not the time or place to deal with them. But at least you won't be pretending that something isn't there.

You'll find we keep coming back to the idea of not pretending. This is not accidental. In order for any kind of connection to take place between you and your audience – and that connection is essential to you delivering something of value – it's is vital that you be authentic. And if you're pretending there's not a parade next door, or you're pretending that there isn't a rhino head on the table, then you're not going to be presenting a very authentic communication.

Fill in the 3 obstacles, whether environmental or attitudinal, that may block your communication.

OBSTACLES
1
2
3

Chapter 10

Value

Now we want to look at the question of Value. We assert that you should provide value in your communication, regardless of whether the audience chooses to do what you want them to do. Let's repeat this because it's really important. Imagine you are speaking to a potential client and you want them to do business with you. But you should, in your communication, give them value. They're going to hear you speak. They're going to have a phone call with you. They're going to have a meeting with you. They're going to receive a letter from you. They're going to read your book. After that communication has taken place you want them to go away from the situation saying, "That was time well spent. I got something out of it." *Even if you never see them again!* And that is the tricky part. The value gets created *whether or not they take the action you want them to take!* You create value whether or not they do business with you. And you create your communication to deliver that value. The shift in thinking here is that this is not about the value your product or service provides. This is only about your communication in this specific situation.

By thinking about this in advance of your communication, it creates a habit of always creating value in your communication.

The value we're talking about here is a "present value." This is different than the opportunity value or "future value" of doing business with you or following the course of action you've directed. This value is not a promise for the future. It is a value to the audience *right* now.

What could that value be? The most obvious one is information. That's the value we're most prone to providing in our communication. Someone now knows something they didn't know before that helps them in their life. Yet that isn't the only value you can create. Value can be insights, seeing something in a way they hadn't before. Having an enjoyable experience. Feeling confident. Being energized or entertained. While the information, insight and ideas you have create value, think beyond that to other ways you can provide value. Expand what you think of as value.

Some examples of the value our clients have shared is:

- Clarified understanding
- Laughed, had fun, been entertained
- Plan for action

- Feel appreciated, understood, heard
- A good process for self management
- Hopeful or optimistic about the future
- A new tool to support them being more balanced in their life
- A new methodology
- Feel better about themselves
- Feel important
- Understand the direction the company is taking
- Know how changes will impact them

While you are focused on creating value in all your communication, you have the right to say when you stop creating value, as in those situations and with those people who will abuse your intent to give by continually taking with no compensation. The idea here is to create "present value" and of course to establish that there is "future value" that you will be compensated for.

Chapter 10 Exercise

Now, in the space below, list the value you will create in the specific communication situation you've selected. All of the things you list should be specific, measurable and concrete. They should be able to withstand the test of "What's in it for me?" and "Why should I care?"

	VALUE
1	
2	
3	

Chapter 11

You

You've probably noticed that up until now this entire book has been like taking a fire hose, putting it up against your ear, and blasting all the stuff out of your head that doesn't work in your communication. Up to now everything has been focused on shifting the attention from you to your audience. Now, finally, we're going to focus on you, the communicator. This is the part where, for once, you get to be the center of your universe. Here we identify who you need to be in your specific communication situation to get the results you want.

The answer is quite simple. Who you need to be is yourself, your *authentic* self. This is not about you pretending to be someone other than who you are. In fact it's the opposite. It is really about you being in connection with who you are. We define our authentic self very narrowly. It starts from when we're little kids. Babies don't have a lot of trouble being fully expressive of who they are. They want something. They cry. They don't like something. They cry. They enjoy something. They giggle. And they don't have a lot of judgment about themselves. That doesn't come until later. That comes when parents impose upon them "good kids don't behave that way."

> "He who knows others is wise. He who knows himself is enlightened"
> – *Lao-Tzu*

Then you go to school. Your friends say "Yuck, those are gross shoes. How come you don't have this kind? You shouldn't be wearing that." It gets worse when you get in high school. Then we have the thoughts "None of the girls or the boys are going to like me unless I do this. Act this way. Wear this. Look that way." Then we start working, with all the pressures to be less and less expressive of our authentic self, to be more conformed into what we think others expect.

We start out as fully expressed human beings and gradually, over time, the box we call ourselves gets smaller and smaller and smaller. By the time we reach this stage of our lives, we're living a very small, confined definition of who we are. And of course we think that this is all that we are. We've often forgotten that there even are other options. In this chapter we want you to get back in contact with the rest of yourself, so that you can present the most appropriate, most effective authentic self to your audience when you're delivering your communication.

And this is not something that we are asking you to do idly. We understand both the importance of this kind of act, as well as the difficulty of doing it. But we ask it because, of all the things we talk about in our workshops or our one-on-one coaching, this one stands out as being central. Why? Because our basic argument is that (and make no mistake this is the meat of the matter) in order to be a really effective communicator; in order to form the connection to your audience that is essential to powerful communication, you have to be yourself. You must be your authentic self. We've said time and again that any kind of fakery gets spotted immediately by your audience and no more quickly and none more devastatingly than being inauthentic.

So far everything we've talked about in this book has been about getting through the clutter and noise that impede everyday communications and really form a connection between you and another person so that what you say gets across. So often in communication what we get is soulless information, cold stats or emotionless requests. We don't get a sense that the person we're hearing or reading cares about us, about our concerns, or even about the information that's being shoved at us.

With a lot of our work we talk about this authentic person as a question of *Being vs. Doing*. It's all a little conceptual but worth understanding to get the philosophy of great communication. Being is literally *who you are* being in a particular moment in time. This is the very essence of your personality, intelligence, wit, joy, anger, experience, belief, understanding, feeling, failures, competence, history, comforts, and fears that come together to form the 'you' that others experience.

We're not naturally inclined to talk about things in these terms. Most of us, if we thought about it at all, would simply say we are who and what we are. That it is an unconscious, uncontrollable state we occupy. We don't usually think of 'being' as an activity – its' a passive state. If you were asked to walk or jump or sit you'd know how to do that, but how do you 'be'? And for most of us it is a passive state, it's something we don't think about and something we don't have a lot of control over. But it changes depending on our mood, our surroundings and a hundred other variables that affect us daily. It's a lot like breathing, we do it naturally and without any thought. But just as we can learn to control our breathing – holding our breath for swimming – so too we can learn to control our being. It takes a bit of practice and effort. But like many of the components of the **Power to Connect** template it's a muscle we already have but which has gone weak. All we need to do is exercise it and get back in shape.

Doing is a bit easier to get our heads around. It is all the stuff, the actions, we do, as a matter of course with our bodies. Let's look at examples of both.

We've seen professional speakers give presentations. They know their material, they give flawless, technically perfect speeches which are timed well, paced appropriately, structured correctly and so on. There's nothing wrong with their presentation or their message. Yet the audience feels something is missing. We don't get a sense of a person there. It's like this zombie has shown up and is doing an impression of the speaker. And everything that makes them interesting and everything that makes them someone you'd want to be in relationship with is missing. And the audience knows something is missing. They may not be able to pinpoint what it is. But they know something's not there.

And here's what's missing: there is no authentic person there. The speaker is all 'doing' and no 'being'. If you try really hard you can almost hear the script running through that speaker's head:

> *Speak slowly for this passage. Stress the main point. Pause. Turn. Refer to notes. Sip water. Look seriously at the audience. Smile – show warmth. Launch into recap. Make eye contact. Turn. Fold hands.*

And so on.

And what's going on is that this person is entirely caught up in doing, in actions, in scripted or off-the-cuff mannerisms and tics that give the impression that there's someone in the front of the room delivering a speech, when in actual fact there isn't. What the audience wants – even if we don't know it – is a connection. A real live human being in front of us, not just transmitting data, but relating to us and having a conversation. The same can be said of someone presenting to a room full of strangers, or someone just having a conversation with a colleague at work. We miss the connection. But when it's there, it works, and we as the audience know it does, and you as the communicator know it does.

The best way to picture this is to imagine the version of yourself that you are with your spouse or best friend. That witty, clever, warm, joyous person that they know and love. That's authenticity. Now imagine being that person in every communication you undertake! Imagine the results your communication will bear.

Now you can see why we believe this to be the foundation of the coaching and communication design work we do. And it's conceptual enough that you can probably understand why we left it to the end of the book to cover.

So now we invite you to think about the ways in which you've been limiting your self-expression. Look at the small box called 'you' that you've been inside of and examine it in context of your communication situation. Look also at your audience. Look at what it is that you want them to remember. How you want them to feel? What you want them to do? What you appreciate about them? What obstacles are in the way? What value do you intend to create? When you've done all this then identify who is it that you need to be to deliver on that. Think of yourself in a more expanded view. Break through whatever that little box you put yourself in and think of yourself outside of that, like the real you. The one you know is inside there. Who do you need to be in order to deliver the goods?

This is not about faking it or acting. This is far more real than most of us have ever experienced.

Some examples:

- Passionate
- Open & caring
- Confident
- An authority
- Clear
- Humorous
- Trustworthy
- Exciting
- Forceful

Turn to your template and write down who you need to be when you deliver your communication. Write down as many as you think are appropriate. Yes you will have to edit them and get it down to a list of three. But for now you really should just brainstorm – this is one activity that most of us are really out of practice at doing.

If you find yourself discarding parts of yourself because "it's inappropriate" look again. That's a big warning bell. Something we've heard many times from financial advisors is, "I can't be humorous. We're talking about money for Heaven's sake!" Look again at how you're limiting yourself. Isn't it possible to be light hearted and serious minded? Of course it is. Many of us have been to funerals where the most touching eulogy was funny and we were laughing through our tears. A truly effective communication where the speaker was not limited by some preconceived nonsense (probably learned in childhood) that sad people shouldn't laugh. Begin to exercise some of those unused self muscles and get them back into shape.

Answer the following questions with the first thing that comes to mind. You will find it insightful in uncovering some parts of yourself that have gone dormant.

Chapter 11 Exercise

1. I was told I should never act ____________________.
2. I could never do ______________________________.
3. Accepted people don't ________________________.
4. People will not think favorably of me if I __________.
5. I secretly wish I were able to ____________________.
6. How I express myself creatively is _______________.
7. I used to express myself creatively by _____________.
8. Things I used to do that I don't anymore are ____.
9. People in my profession would never ____.
10. If I won the lottery I would ____________________.
11. The last thing these people want to hear is _______.

Now fill in the following blanks with who do you need to be, without limiting yourself.

	YOU
1	
2	
3	

Chapter 12

Conclusion

Throughout this book we've been aiming at one goal: improving our communication. If you are someone who, for whatever reason, saw an opportunity to improve the results you are getting with your communication then this book will serve as a good template for designing communication that works.

There is no formula for how the communication, letter, chat, email, presentation, sermon, interview or eulogy will play out. But there is a template for planning your communication that will allow you to create clear and effective communication that delivers on the results you're looking for. With The **Power to Connect** we've recognized that human communication works the way it does and that nothing we do will change that. So rather than work against it, we've created a system that works with human habit and tendency to create powerful communication. When it comes to communication, we've found that it makes much more sense to ride the horse in the direction it's going.

The **Power to Connect**, as we've said before, is not the power to talk to someone. It's the power to create immediate, significant connections between you and the people you wish to communicate with. Because that connection is the basis for effective communication. To begin to create this connection you must know your audience. If you don't know who you are speaking or writing to then what is the likelihood that anything you say will be of any relevance to them? Not very high. So the first step in designing a communication is to know who you will be communicating to. An architect must know the family he is designing a home for, and so too you should know who you're speaking to.

We're not talking about surface level stuff necessarily. That's a good place to start but we need to dig deeper. That's why we strive to understand as much as we can about the people we're communicating to. Because who they are will naturally lead us to what they want, what they're concerned about, what they need, fear, desire, strive for and dream of. Once we know this we can begin to understand what filters they're using.

In communication we all use filters. We all seek to understand the barrage of information we're being presented with daily. That's why our brain filters information. And all of our filters can be reduced to two questions that our brain asks of everything we experience: What's in it for me? And Why should I care?

Everybody always uses these two questions to sort out the massive amount of information they have to contend with (information you as a communicator are competing with by the way). So when you as a communicator are designing communications why not, if you already know they're asking these two questions, give them the answers. This is not about fooling anyone. It's the opposite. It's walking into the exam with the answers to the questions. Only this time it's not cheating.

By this point in our communication design we've begun to suspect something pretty essential to The **Power to Connect** – that it really isn't about us. So much of human communication takes place in the receiver's head and heart, not in the speaker's mouth. How we receive information, how much of it we take in, what we do with it, how we act on it are all things which take place in the audience's world not ours.

So knowing this, we took a look at designing communication to interact with and ultimately have effect on those things. The things that as communicators we don't normally pay attention to, or have much to do with. We ask ourselves what three things do we want our audience to remember. There's a lot of work here to boil down your information so that you are clear that of all the things you'll say or write that the three most important salient pieces are clear in your head and clear in theirs.

Another aspect of communication that takes place entirely in the audience's experience is what they feel about what we have just communicated. This is an element that we simply have no clue about as a matter of course. We're embarrassed or confused by the fact that as humans, even in a business situation or environment, we are still emotional creatures. But we are, and again given that your audience is going to have an emotional reaction to what you have to say or write, wouldn't it be a prudent thing to think, ahead of time, about what you'd like that reaction to be? Of course it would. Just as it would be prudent to consider what you'd like the audience to do when they leave the room.

A surprising number of communicators forget, or fudge the call to action. This is fancy talk for WHAT'S NEXT. We phrase it as "Who will do what by when" But either way it's another moment where your clarity will go a long way to the effectiveness of your communication. And remember this is your communication, so if you don't know what you want them to do next then they certainly won't know.

These three elements are essential. If you don't know what you want your audience to do, how you want them to feel or even what you want them to walk out of the room with in terms of a memory, then how can you possibly expect they will? The more clear we are with this stage, the better and more focused our communication will be. All of the communications we are designing and delivering have a purpose, we're not just talking to hear the sound of our own voices. If what we have to say is worth saying then there has to be an outcome we envision as a result of it. The clearer we are about our criteria, what we want them to feel, remember and do next, then the more clear our communication will be and naturally more effective it will be.

That's all about what we are going to say. We also need to spend a bit of time talking about what we're not going to say. Study after study have told us that a huge amount of human communication takes place non-verbally. Whether it's posture, tone or eye contact there are many ways in which we subtly transmit and receive.

As a quotation we used earlier in the book says *"What we say is important for in most cases the mouth speaks what the heart is full of".* So it's a good idea to look at what kind of baggage we are bringing with us to the communication? This is a section that many people like to gloss over, it can be a bit uncomfortable but in equal measure it is valuable. One way get to the bottom of what we're thinking and unconsciously communicating is to look at first all the negative things we're holding onto when we are designing and delivering a communication (usually about the people we're communicating to but it could be about what we're saying) and replace those things with the kinds of positive, appreciative sentiments that will serve us for effective communication. Not by making stuff up, but by choosing to focus on the more positive aspects of the people we're speaking to and the information we're discussing.

In a perfect world this would set us up for delivering a fantastic (and effective) communication. But of course things don't always go as planned. We live in a flawed world and that sometimes will interfere with our communication. So in a surprising – but logical – step, we plan for those obstacles. We sit down and list everything that could go wrong, everything that, in fact, *will* go wrong, and we solve it before we get anywhere near to delivering the communication.

At this point we are putting together some pretty amazing communications and we're pretty well prepared to deliver them. But there's always room for improvement. The **Power to Connect** is very much concerned with every communication we design and deliver being powerful and effective. And one of the most effective ways to do that is to add value – present, unconditional value. So that our audience walks away knowing that the time spent with you has added something to their lives.

And in the end, after all the homework is done and the preparation is complete. When we know who we're talking to, what we want them to remember, feel and do next. When we are delivering our communication from a place of appreciation for our audience, when we are working with and around the obstacles we are facing and when we know we are presenting great value to our audience there is only one thing left to consider. And that is *Who are we being!* Who are we being in relation to the information we're presenting, the people we're speaking to, even in relation to ourselves will affect how well we deliver our communication. We consider, and list, all the attributes of ourselves that we need to bring into the room with us when we're presenting this communication.

This is hard work. As we've said before it's not meant to be taken as theory. That would be interesting and informative. Instead we mean this book to be a workbook. It's a template and a guide for you to put together communications each and every time you set out to, that deliver the results you want. We expect that you will use this book not just for the communication you've been designing this time but every time you want to create a truly remarkable communication.

You can do more templates and keep them all together so that you can keep track of the communications you're designing and begin to see which muscles are getting stronger and which ones need work.

As you use this book again and again the principals here will become second nature, you'll find yourself zipping through the steps in your head on the drive to the clients and so on. The template makes a good checklist for making sure that you've covered everything you need to before having a conversation, writing a letter, chatting on the phone.

When a communication doesn't deliver on the results you declared, you can use the template to check the work you've done – often you'll find that you can identify the source of the difficulty fairly quickly and get to correcting it for your next communication.

When we're about to go into a client meeting we'll often have little pre-meeting huddles to cover the template. "Okay we're pitching a huge client on a new piece of business, what do we need to do here, who do we need to be, what do we appreciate about this client, who do we need to be, what do we want them to feel, remember and do next, what obstacles are we facing...?" It's become second nature for us and an incredibly effective tool for structuring our communications with friends, family, colleagues, clients, employees and just the people we interact with daily to become more effective and get the results we want.

We've written this book because we know this works. This isn't something we made up while removed from the real world. This is the stuff we do for a living every day. We work with our clients to create communication that is effective – by measures they create. The **Power To Connect** has been culled from thousands of hours of work, hundreds of coaching sessions and dozens of workshops over our nearly a half century of combined experience.

Get in the habit of using this template every time you plan communications and stay in the practice of it. Identify some of the communications situations that you'll you be facing in the next week, pick three that you are interested in having particularly good results in, and use this template to design those communications.

Our intention is that the **Power to Connect** Template becomes as valuable to you as to the many people who've already begun using it and who've made it part of their regular communication design. We are happy to get this chance to share our lives' work with you.

THE POWER TO CONNECT®
WORKSHEET

Communication situation: ______________________________

Date: ______________________________

THEM	APPRECIATE
1	1
2	2
3	3

REMEMBER	OBSTACLES
1	1
2	2
3	3

FEEL	VALUE
1	1
2	2
3	3

DO	YOU
1	1
2	2
3	3

Endnote

[i] The D.O.S. worksheet is an especially powerful asset for those who's communication is directed toward clients and potential clients. Dan Sullivan is the creator of this tool and many others. Information on the work of Dan Sullivan and The Strategic Coach can be found at http://www.strategiccoach.com. Or at 800-387-3206 or 888-872-8877.

Corporate Vision Communications Workshops & Services

Power To Connect® Workshops

Take the power of this book to the next level. This one-day workshop gives you an opportunity to get personal coaching from the authors. You will work with the **Power to Connect** Template in a variety of communication situations. Each participant will prepare for their most important upcoming opportunity. You will leave the session confident and well prepared to get great results.

Bravo Presentation Coaching®

For those who have achieved a high level of success and understand that achieving more depends on superb presentation and speaking skills. Bravo Presentation Coaching is a comprehensive, intensive workshop that will give you a thorough understanding of communication strategy, structure, content development and delivery. You will practice and receive coaching and feedback from leading communications experts.

Strategy First

Strategy First is the foundation of Corporate Vision's proven approach to marketing communication. Strategy First is a four-module system designed to improve the efficiency and results of your marketing and sales efforts. Each module is guaranteed to deliver specific result in a defined period of time.

Corporate Vision Special Projects

There are times when you know it has to be done right, when you're launching a new product or planing a critical meeting – when your business success depends on it.

Our Emmy Award winning creative team is available to create and execute your, PowerPoint, video or web project. We promise fresh ideas that are on strategy every time.

Guest Speaker

Teresa Easler is available to speak to your group, company or organization. Her speaking style is characterized by strong content, clearly presented with energy and fun. She is known for making a solid personal connection with her audience. Topics focus on personal communication, strategies for improving marketing and sales and the art and science of being an entrepreneur.

For more information check out the Corporate Vision website http://www.cvcomm.com or give us a call at 416-696-2020.

Corporate Vision Communication Inc.
1440 Don Mills Road, Suite 100
Toronto, Ontario
M3B 3M1

Notes